Here and Hereafter

Here and Hereafter

POEMS BY ELTON GLASER

THE UNIVERSITY OF ARKANSAS PRESS

FAYETTEVILLE

2005

Library of Congress Cataloging-in-Publication Data

Glaser, Elton.
Here and hereafter : poems / by Elton Glaser.
p. cm.
ISBN 1-55728-796-1 (pbk. : alk. paper)
I. Title.
PS3557.L314H47 2005
811'.54—dc22
2005007123

for Bob and Anita Muzik

Home may be where the heart is but it's no place to spend Wednesday afternoon.

—WALKER PERCY

I travel within myself as in a country unknown, even though I have traversed it many times.

—GUSTAVE FLAUBERT

Acknowledgments

I am grateful to the editors who accepted many of these poems for publication in their magazines, sometimes in slightly different form:

"Next Time Around," *Artful Dodge;* "Café Voltaire," *Cincinnati Poetry Review;* "Down to Earth," *The Comstock Review;* "By the Waters of Babylon," *Crab Orchard Review;* "Home for Old Gods" and "On or about the Feast of Saint Absentia," *Dogwood;* "Postcards from Iberia," *Ellipsis;* "Half-Numb from Winter, on a Morning Almost Warm," *Field;* "Solstice of the Goat," *The Gettysburg Review;* "Lake Effect," *Hayden's Ferry Review;* "Madonnas at Ca' d'Oro," *Hunger Mountain Review;* "Plotting the Lines," *Italian Americana;* "In the Zone of Perpetual Weather," *The Journal;* "Venice," *The Laurel Review;* "Home Truths," *The Ledge;* "Crab Festival in Henderson, Louisiana," *Louisiana Literature;* "Meditation in Blue and White," *The Marlboro Review;* "The Runes, the Brute Remedies," *Meridian;* "Blue Passports," *Mid-American Review;* "Between Matins and the Late Alarm" and "Blizzard near Emporia, 1893," *The Missouri Review;* "Dozing through Italy," *North Dakota Quarterly;* "Here and Hereafter," "Latter Days," "Low and Delicious," "Post-partum Blues," and "Twenty-First of June," *Poetry;* "After Bonnard," *Poetry Northwest;* "Heroic Roses," *River Styx;* "Escape Velocity," *Southern Poetry Review;* "Evenings at the Coconut Hotel," *The Wallace Stevens Journal.*

"*Calendario da Firenze*" was published in *The Age of Koestler,* ed. Nicolaus Kogon (Kalamazoo, MI: Practices of the Wind, 1994).

"Crab Festival in Henderson, Louisiana" was reprinted in *O Taste and See: Food Poems,* ed. David Garrison and Terry Hermsen (Huron, OH: Bottom Dog Press, 2003).

A few of these poems, especially the Italian pieces, were made possible by fellowships from the National Endowment for the Arts and the Ohio Arts Council and by sabbatical leave from the University of Akron.

Contents

Here and Hereafter

From a Heaven Not Mine to Lose

This light in midmorning, at the rise of June,
Coming down through the thick Ohio trees,
Seems to say: Honey, you can't be too rich or too thin.

It speaks in my own voice, a drawl inside the clear
Vernacular of Akron, and looks as much October
As late spring, leaning both ways, as I do,

Two seasons in one shine, a rush and lure of light,
With no eager innocence and no mistake: a day
That says what it means, even in split speech.

It falls without favor on a proud robin
Swaggering around, lord and master of the worms,
And on the sad knowing nod of roses when the wind lifts,

And would pour over me, too, if I were not
Reading in my easy chair, only now looking up, wrenched
Awry by the ruins of another bent sentence,

To see this light that never moves a leaf
But alters everything, both of us foreign and at home
In my tongue of odd American, my mongrel sublime.

Eclogue from the Back Forty

What brings you here, Tu Fu, among the horses
Grazing their way through a spring rain, hides

Steaming like mist off a river? Far from home
And the dry rubble of your hut, exile

From another war, another drunken empire of sorrow,
You're an old man again, your bamboo cane

Slashing a poem in the heavy dirt, then
Smearing it out with wine from a clay jar, until

You're the only Chinese character around.
Or not even that. Do I imagine you,

A gust of white wind in the rough pasture?
The horses seem to think so, this evening of

Mud and thunder, plunging their sleek enormous heads
Up and down, a storm between earth and air,

And flinging from their thick manes
A million silver glints across the dark.

Low and Delicious

—the fire, the sweet hell within,
The unknown want, the destiny of me.

—WALT WHITMAN

This morning, even the roses look morose,
More elegy than awe. And yet,
The sun holds up its end of the bargain, rays
Gilding the grass and the green thorns,
Midas with a clumsy touch, until
Everything we love grows stiff and cold.
But that's spring for you, late spring,
Like a man with no sense of humor
Making jokes, and the hand-me-down eye
Always sizing up the day
One season behind the evidence.
So charity begins in misgiving, or ought to;
So faith and hope have their own ambitions,
Sucking up to the absolute: the eternal
Spawned by desperation, sweet nothings
Whelped out of fear. Or perhaps,
With an ear for anger, a nose for
The rituals of rot, I'm just too good
At writing the strophes of catastrophe,
Scriptures in a pickled idiom
For the slow torment of the middle class,
When all I really want is

A plate of bacon in a fracas of eggs
At some little diner in Hinckley, Ohio,
Where every year, before the blood warms,
The buzzards come home to roost.

Cusp of the Halcyon, Threshold of Dew

No one would call this
The stale of April, even though
We've seen it all before—

Early pearls of the snowdrop, crocus
In its false cheer, the day
Half sun and half disaster—

As no one would mind the wind
Blowing on some Italian table
The old aromas of Rome.

And you feel it, too, an air
Dead so long it lives again—
Breath freshened from the grave,

Flowers by the headstone, and birds
Pouring out from the maple trees
The new syrup of their song,

As if they saw Persephone
At the cusp of the halcyon, her heel
On the threshold of dew.

Time to turn the earth; time
To pick the litter from the backyard,
Stick and cone and junk,

Fallen leaves of the calendar,
The ruins of winter on which we build
A green season from sap and seed.

Thunder at noon: an awkward poise
Of bells, the Easter steeple
Bringing down the heavy hymns,

Tongues from the brass of resurrection
That echo in the oaken aisles,
In the white throats of lilies.

Out here, we name the lean infants
Coming back from the cold,
In the garden and on the bent boughs,

As far from frost as from
A late summer so obese
It seems anonymous, a night

Shattered in stars, a swollen moon.
Between these poles, high heat and high ice,
The blood finds its balance.

Now grass stands up on its wet stems.
A bear rises from a savage sleep.
The glass of sky shines bulletproof.

This paradise preserved by instinct, by the naked
Touch of the primitive,
Troubles the compass and the grandfather clock.

It frets the invisible, the pure silence that
Jewels itself in vacancy, but welcomes
Our hands buried in the warm dirt

Down to the wrist and root—
This quick in the ancient cradle,
This world that weathers everything.

After Bonnard

Dachshunds and nudes and the little sitting room
That gave on the garden, both doors open,
French doors in a French house on the Côte d'Azur,
Slick of the mirror like the sea's warm slide,
And the old man with his rags and brushes,
Canvas tacked to the wall, a world of colors
That stroked themselves in a hard haze of blue
And the yellow of light and lemons, deep red
In a dress or a cupboard's back, and on the table
Red felt under bowls of blossom and fruit—

If you were there, posed at some early hour
Where the steep steps rose in stone to the almond tree,
Or in a bath just drawn, lean breasts
Eased up above the water line, and the tiles
Cool and smooth where the small dog lay,
Sprays of mimosa floating near the wide window,
Even the old man would feel in his flesh
Blood beating like a bell, and put down his tools
For the look of you, hair shining, paint still wet,
Bare eyes in praise of everything they touch.

Blue Passports

Spare me the spare: no January winds
Stripping the tinsel from dead trees.

I'll take the messy opulence of spring,
Mudsong and birdsong and long trumpets of the sun.

If I'm down to one day, make it
A Tuesday in April, and some little hill town

In Tuscany, rough wine in the glasses
And a luster of tall air along the stones,

And you there with me, for a late meal
Of capers in seasalt and wild boar,

Two pilgrims in the candlebloom
Before the pagan ceremonies of the bed.

We're traveling on blue passports
To the country of desire,

Which, on every map, is always
Deep pink.

Next Time Around

Some things seem so hard to imagine,
You might as well leave them
To the pros. Just what I was thinking
About Jesus in Ohio, a state where
They like their corn homegrown
And their supper in neutral shades:
Jesus in Cleveland, Jesus in Marietta,
And Jesus in between, stepping out
Of the gospels and the simple hymns,
Goodyear sandals on His feet, making
Tracks down a dirt road as if
He still could hear some farmer's bark
At His bare heels: *Come off that cross,*
Boy, and help me slop the swine.
But what do I know? I've never
Seen the Virgin on a barn side
Or scripted my vision of the universe
For a cable show. Maybe that's not
The way it would happen at all.
Maybe He'd find His agony
As a day trader in Columbus
Or as left tackle for the Browns.
Maybe He'd hitch himself
To the Amish, who look good in black,
Or buy a winery in the boondocks

And turn those sour grapes into
A snooty little chardonnay.
Foster son of the buckeyes, amateur
Of the muses, I've probably got it
All wrong. Why would a God
Keep coming back, like reruns
After the local news? And why Ohio,
Where the people already feel so pious
They put their pennies, one by one,
In the Sunday collection plate
And their dreams of sex under
The counters of convenience stores.
It's a mystery to me, even more
Than my dull mind can handle
On a slow day, though I keep wondering
How He'd stack up here, among
The crowded churches and the empty
Steel mills, buying His chain burgers
And fries from a drive-in and His cocktails
At some boutique saloon in the suburbs.
And what chance He'll be coming soon?
At these odds, you might as well
Play the lottery. Or maybe I'm mistaken—
Somebody wins it big most every week.
Still, I can't say I've seen
Any wisemen whipping their tired camels
Along the turnpike. And God knows,
It's a long wet walk across Lake Erie,
No matter how you multiply the fish.

Between Matins and the Late Alarm

It must be morning: I can hear the birds
Bitching at each other, or else some cat's around,
Sly enough to make them squeal.

Thank God the angels play harps
And not banjos. Who'd want to wake each day
To breakdowns in heaven, steel reels for the cloudhoppers?

Must I rise, as the sun does, busy and ambitious,
Or can I model myself
On the laidback horizon, that latitude I long for?

Last night, thunder with both barrels at full bore,
And buckshot of rain rattling the roof.
Even the stars kept their heads down, their eyes closed.

I slept through lightning and gutterfloods,
My body twitching like some
Deranged baby of middle age, suckled on nightmares.

And now, past dawn in late spring,
Air smooth and warm around me, as if I were
Swaddled in suede,

A quick of sudden peace, silence in which
I could mouth my early prayers—
But to whom? And for what?

Must I ease out of bed again
On the wrong side of life, and walk into morning
With one blue sock, one black?

Up, says the robin. *Up*, screams the jay.
It's a fight to the last feather, until the cat's
Got your tongue.

Shake off this queasy sleep. The day's
Already racing down the flowerheads, only
One short step to the frost.

Café Voltaire

That dark man next to me, both hands
Brooding on his cognac, intones:

Like the turtle who strolls
Under its own tureen, I'm
In the soup again.

Of course, it sweetens in his tongue.
Everything does—the words give off
Something of honey
And the brisk ricochet of bees.

And, of course, it's spring—
The beech so slick with rain
In the gray evening, it looks
Wrapped in moleskin; and the women slender
As those small trees by the sidewalk,
A figment of leaves
On the nude branches, half-awake,
Still trembling in the wind.

I miss the *chk chk chk* of grackles,
Fifty-three stations blue on the rigged TV,
A voice that purrs my name
With every pillowed syllable in place.

I miss the easy thrills of innocence,
Like a cheerleader sucking
The salt from french fries
After a hard day of failing tests.

And when that man, wringing
The damp droop of his mustache, begins
A frank exchange on snails
Purged in their fat shells, on money
And the miseries of romance,

I count the coins out
And step into the late March dark
Where the windows patch
A warm blur on the pavement,

My face ghostly in the glass,
Pale eyes fastened to
All that's foreign, midway
Through the journey and still
Outside the outside.

Escape Velocity

Little sail of the sundial, tacking into shadow
As the light shifts, what cargo do you carry
Out beyond the breakers and the sliding foam?

All those hours I've wasted down the dark years
Pool up behind me, slag and poisons of the past.
There's no use waiting for some freak season when

Fifty daffodils will rise from ice like a solar flare,
Not with this sun sickening away. And it's far too late
For one more clammy miracle in the straw and dung.

Among the rusty nouns, I'm greasing the verbs of
Desire and retrieval, running my tongue to a sleek speed,
Quicker than quick, until I'm down to nothing flat.

Home for Old Gods

Who knows why they came here, or why
I let them in? Lares and Penates:
Small gods of the mirror and the tennis shoe,
Gods who keep the knife sharp, who test
The bathwater with a toe as soft as clouds
They once walked on, anonymous gods
The Romans forgot to name, laid off
Since the last invasion, pinkslipped
From the pantheon. Others may worship
Spirits of the tree and stone, the river deities,
Lords of the harvest and heavy swine.
But these old ones earn their keep, more like
Bashful janitors than victims underfoot,
With no grudge against silence or solitude,
Barely there, a silhouette in ruins, pale
As a nightlight, with a faint falsetto
Like a simmer of gnats. I see them only
In the brightwork of copper pots, dazzle
Of a glass gone numb with dry martinis.
However far they're fallen, they don't pout
Around the household or piss in the pea soup.
Am I priest or disciple, servant or master?
I pour out the morning bowl of libation,
Coffee so black I can almost trace
A blurred penumbra going down. And I

Never mind when something's missing or
Moved around—widow of the silk sock,
Car keys hung on a curtain rod. You can
Say this house is haunted, a restless home
For tutelary spooks, but the gods inside
Have given me more time, more grit,
More reason to write these busy hymns
In praise of everything I don't believe.

Plotting the Lines

> Was it, in short, ever well to be elsewhere when one
> might be in Italy?
>
> —EDITH WHARTON

I'm traveling down the map, from that
Wet wedge in the higher
Thigh of Italy,

Until I hit
The kneecap of Rome, like some
Mafia *brutto* with a grudge against the ruins,

And not this tourist that I am, cross-eyed and lost
In the gutters of five guidebooks.
I dream my way

Along the cool lakes, and up the hills of every
Tuscan town, and through
The death-wish traffic in the capital—

Time to move now,
At the ratchet of another cranky year,
The mind losing traction, panic in the blood.

Let me set my sore feet
Among the goats and vines and villas,
By stone revetments on the shore,

And in the dark cathedrals and academies,
Where wall and canvas
Give back the look by which we see.

I'm planning a spring plane
To that metropolis of unconstructed silk and faux fur,
Our first night

North and a train away,
On the gardenous waters of Como, and then
The slow rails to a sinking city,

The light rising
From pole to palace, carried by
The black boats of fantasy,

And on to the dome, the dull river
Where Dante lived,
Hammer and chisel of the rustic sun,

And up the coast to the palm trees
Of Rapallo, Pound's town,
Campari and soda on the rooftop table,

And in the park a statue of Columbus
Fingering the West, stool pigeon
Under the pigeonshit,

Before the last stop where all roads lead,
Layer on layer,
The streets abuzz with girls on motorbikes,

Sleek and abrupt,
Or with old mothers from the south,
Long shadow of a shawl

Over wrinkle and whisker, their shoes
Hoofclops on the cobblestone,
A city so deep

That every shovel uncovers
The dirt of antiquity,
Remnants of an empire reckless and overruled

—No safety pins on a toga—
And the bones on which basilicas were built,
Pagan or papal,

And even now
The air of sweet permission, pleasures far beyond
The olive and the olive skin,

Never mind
The hard biscotti, espresso thick and bitter,
Like an oil slick on the tongue,

Or a pocketful of someone else's knuckles,
Or the lean felonious cats—
Ah, Italia,

You've made me
A leg man late in my years, believing
Every legend on the map.

Evenings at the Coconut Hotel

They had come for fire, for barbarous waters
And the blood of sun, nothing so subtle
As this gold and mauve, this lavender,
This rose muting a slate blue. They could
Blame it on the season, or the false brochures,
Or the bloom of clouds that open
Like late hibiscus in the terra cotta pots,
But not themselves, not when the day's expense
Ends in a tonic of desire, a sweating glass
Held against the sky and sea, through which
They saw the heavens settle in a calm of stars,
The moon among them, and so much light
Immaculate on the white cloth and crystal,
On the bone plates, such brilliance rising
From the terrace tiles, they felt as if they sat
Inside the pure approval of a diamond, cool and clear,
And called the waiter for another drink.

Meditation in Blue and White

1

It wasn't what he wanted, this moonlight
Sugaring oblivion, and white gulls that cried
The night sea up the beaches, like ghosts of crows.
It wasn't a world so dark his eye
Denied all consolations of the sun, so dumb
The suck and scrape of waves along the sand would
Vanish in his ear, enormous and nothing, until
His mind, in the pure cast metal of itself,
Went on ringing and ringing alone, halfway between
The bride's bouquet and flowers on the catafalque,
Bell in the still balance of the real.

2

Philosopher of the absent shore, deprivation's darling,
Assassin of the blood senses, cold namer
In the warm elysium, gone bald from
A tight riot of thoughts, a murderous mob
Clamoring against the inside of the skull,
With a beard part pitch, part salt, almost
Canceling the mouth, the lips that look still starved
For bread and kisses, for cups purpled with burgundy,
Even the lean shadows won't please you, unless
They fall on snow, drifts of it, bonemeal and ash
From everything that winter burned away.

3

Fans in the summer cottage above the beach
Stir up the youngest air of memory, bringing in
Odors of wild grape and dune grass. The sailboats don't fly
The acid flags of apocalypse; they ride
A slick of savage sunlight down the late waters.
It wasn't what he wanted, so blue a breath
He could feel the day inside him, the sea in his veins.
It was not the nakedness he craved, a thin perpetual peace,
But bare waves of bodies dolphined in the foam,
A sky of gold glints and wind, and gulls
Above the spray, in a squall of their own making.

Calendario da Firenze

for Bob Pope

Soft March, and the wind that lifts
The leaves, bleached leaves, blows them back
Transparent to the branches,
  the cold eccentric bark,
Sap starting under the dry trunks . . .
And something's rising, too,
Through this foreign leaf, this page
Where seven columns hold up
The days divided into now and the longed-for life
  that labors out of reach,
The past closed out
Behind a barricade of crosses; and rising
To that woman reborn from
  Venere e Marte,
The cuppable breast of Sandro's Venus,
Her hair a braided noose
That shades into the neckline of her dress
And splays the unkempt curls
  sidelong on silk,
The planes of her face
Angled upwards to the brow, a second
Dome of Florence that can shun
Seduction and seduce
  by its chaste grace,

No peace for Mars
Or for these eyes that
Glide lightly over her, not
With the expert's beveled gaze
Or the cruel convulsions of de Sade,
But as in April
When the first cricket warms itself
   on its own gaunt song.

Twenty-First of June

The yellow elegies of spring
Burned up in the heat
Weeks ago, dead

Before their time. And now
It's official. I lay this
Wreath of words

On the rose; I throw a handful
Of dirt on the dirt.
The green shoots,

The rootlings brave in snow,
Grow fat and lazy now,
And the big trees

Bulge with birds, a leafquake
Of wind and raw song,
Piping hot.

The season's just begun, and already
I can smell the seeping
Wounds of pinebark,

Air that blisters in the sun;
Already I can feel
The sweat

Slide down the face of summer and
Pool in the steamy streets.
Whatever's ahead of us,

I don't want to know. Just let me
Sit here in the shade
And listen to

The small talk of the rain.

Boy in Alabama

for Rodney Jones

All summer, the high pines sway over you, and honeysuckle
Lags from fence and trunk, sweet filaments in the slow day.
Who was that bird singing to, behind a lattice of thin boughs?
Cheer-up, cheer-up, cheer-up, and then the gone gray wings.

Inside its tangled banks, the little stream pushes itself
Past snag and sandbar. Cool to your ankles in this heat,
You wait for something to arrive, as if the far waters could
Bring you news of who you are, standing here, looking up

As clouds drowse their way somewhere only the wind knows,
While the sky stays at home and lets it all happen:
First blue, then darker, then a black enamel
Cracked with stars and the ruins of a dead moon.

How could night have come so fast? No one's cleared away
Dishes from the supper table or turned up the evening radio.
The dog whines beyond the screen door. You fill his bowl
And watch that poor lean hound fatten on the scraps.

Amateur Sunset, Lake Pontchartrain

Wherever the easel stood, it must have
Rocked in the wind like a broken wave;
And the hand, too, troubled by gusts, judging from
The roughhouse clouds, the smudge of gulls—
Everything inside the frame at sea.

And those flecks near the shoreline: mullets
In a bony leap, or the veer of accident,
The brush disrupted by a tendon's twitch
Or a sudden bubbling from the gut? Or just
A stir of insects in the wet paint?

On either edge, oaks and mimosa
Pose against the low horizon
Like trees in drag, the trunks leaning
On the stiff air, a wallow of boughs
Paralyzed by each swollen stroke.

And the grizzled harmonies of sky and sun:
Hot red of hatred pasted on
The pale grays of compromise, as if
Those soft hairs sipping at a tint
Could fret the heavens to an opulent apocalypse.

The lake's in brown and green, a fuss
Of camouflage; and past the shaken ranks,
A far leveling of swells, smooth as
A stretched belly where a new life kicks,
Scumble from the underside of a thumb.

And those ropy boats beyond the chop—
Why, in such calm, do they heave and plunge?
In their own spray, the sails cut through
The oily waters, canvas on canvas,
Drenched in the swank of some excited eye.

Traveler's Guide to Dining Alone

Perhaps, in your innocence, you dreamed
Of a small table on a rooftop terrace,
Moonlight and lobster and a white
Freshet of wine from the Andes,
Napkin as crisp as a hundred-dollar note,

But not this dark corner
Near the kitchen door, close enough to hear
Tantrums among the *sauciers* and busboys,
Tosspots hawking in the soup du jour.

Perhaps, in your fantasies, yearning
For silver and chandeliers, a menu
Of glamorous names in a silkier tongue,
You feasted on such marvels and revelation
(Soufflé like a sigh, and Tuscan mushrooms
Snuffled up by the chef's own pig; or a rump of
Wildebeest marinated in lion's milk)
That you could taste them all the way down
From the palate to your patella,

Far beyond this stump of candle and a crusty plate,
High-water marks on the stemware, a serving of
Iceberg butter for the hand-me-down rolls,
And sweetbreads like the privates of a gnome.

Now all the plans and pleasures of a languid meal
Collapse to a list of dishes pared down
For some relentless Lent, a no-star night
In a rancid heaven, and every craving
Killed in a cheap collision of beer and Brie.

May we recommend the best course for those
Dining alone: sole, that flat bottom-feeder,
With a snarky little glass of *Chateau du Pissoir*?

And to speed the hours between
The last morsel and the late bill, please bring
A book with you, preferably in leather, and perhaps
The medium-rare edition of those fragments
Left over from the final play
By Esophagus, that hungry Greek:
The great lost tragedy of banquets and blood.

And in Acadia, You

In deep Louisiana, the rivers speak French,
Even that broad slur, the Mississippi, curving
Its tongue around New Orleans.

Barefoot, and with the sun
Summering your naked head, you take off
Your dark glasses, and let the glare gild each ripple.

Above the current, the fisherbirds
Spike down in a glint of scale and talon,
In a loose scatter of skiffs,

And rise again, a ravishing
Cry of shadows
That pour over the sliding swell.

Rapture has its own hard voice, and catchwords
More foreign than the water's
Easy silk of syllables.

And you, whom desire has made
Fluent in wet words, can you stand and answer
From the slippery banks?

Dozing through Italy

Somehow the hum and slow sway of the train
Have eased the summer in,
And my eyes close over
A lifetime of late arrivals. I want
To lie down outside the flux, half-sleeping
In vineyards where shadows pool
Under green panels of the grape leaves,
Holding back a sun that staggers
The spiced air and overcomes us
Like drums pounding out
Music for a broken consort.

But I'm too tired to turn back
These railside rows of corn
Nodding and crowding in
Like bankrupt farmers in Iowa, the dead center
Of that land I buried beneath me
For the first time; and I'm tired
From braving the midnight passage
Miles up through ocean air, strapped down beside
An old man coming home to Palermo
Where the sea slops in, his every breath
An epic of money and emigrant grit, his lips
Still dreaming in the foreign dawn;
And I'm tired as that woman

Traveling against me, silent
As if I'd forced her from
Her birthright of burgers and rooted speech
To the last unplumbed outpost of loneliness.

And then a steely backbeat on the tracks
Speeds up the afternoon, and I blink
In the hot windows, the sour wind,
Waking at forty to another life
Halfway between grief and longing—
As, in the fields veering away from me
Somewhere past Verona, the great
Stately wheels of hay
Have rolled to a sudden stop.

Lake Effect

Pewter this morning, and shadows,
Half the lake
Missing, and half holding its shape
In soft metal still running in scales, in ripples,
Waver polished and plain
As those fish we saw under the float
Yesterday at noon, looking up
At our faces over the edge, six inches
Long and away from us,
Not spooked and not moving, the clouds
Above us and the mud below,
Until we broke
The water in a million scraps, all of them
Coming together again
After the plunge, the vanishing, the pressure
Of the held breath, pawing our way
Through the deep cling of the invisible,
Towards that shore where
Mothers, wading among the children, watched
For some horror to rise,
Even in the shallows at their feet.

Hot Enough for Me

Summer, swollen in its skin, and half-asleep,
Lolls in a trance of sun,
No shadows anywhere.

Once more a month behind the season,
Always late, always
Lazy in the vacant day,

I'm overtaken by July, undone
By all that's left undone,
Perpetual noon of the paralyzed hours.

~

Three times I've planted the annuals, and twice,
Or more, I've watched them die,
One zinnia still grinning with its bucktooth bloom,

A tub of pink impatiens
Nodding in the pine shade, as if they'd come from crops
Grown by the zombie farmers of Catatonia.

Tomatoes, leggy in the heat,
Lean inside their wire hoops, tired from the suckers
That drain them like

The roofing crews and all-purpose repairmen
I pay each week
To make my home a private hell.

~

On the broad back of the pork roast, I lash
Big sprigs of rosemary
From my own worked earth. In a pot of penne,

I stir the first pressing
Of imported oil, virgins sacrificed on a Tuscan hill,
And a handful of rude oregano,

And the flat leaves of parsley in a rough cut.
Over the mozzarella, sliced,
And the red flesh of Early Girls ripened at the stake,

I drip the sweet sting of vinegar,
Cooped up ten years in a wooden cask, and a chrism of olives
Gone green, gone gold, and basil to waken the taste.

Herbs still curling from the stem
Only a few fresh minutes ago: I feel them speak to me,
Eternal Italian on the tongue.

~

Summer afternoon, and somewhere in the neighborhood,
Sinatra sings the wind my way, breezy
As the bright cotton glowing on your thighs, a second skin

More floral than the first. And what do I want
Among the inducements of this day?
The sundress, the sandals, the loose buttons . . .

I want the fever of your hand,
Migrating nightly under the light sheets, and my breath
    coming
In asthmatic rapture, and my face

Deep in the secrets of
Mango and honey and musk. And after the heat,
A tonsure of snow on the mountain top . . .

~

In my chambray workshirt, my khakis
Still patched with mud,
Down on my knees among the weedlings

And the volunteers, seeds windborne or birdborne,
I put my garden in order,
Another Adam after the apple, backache and sweat and dead
    roots.

I pull the broken rake
Through pinestraw, and unlock from the oak
The writhing manacles of ivy,

And snap from the tree of heaven
The false tropic of its fronds.
I shake the hose

Down to the flowerbeds and screw
The sprinkler in, high spray stuck on the upright, water
Watering itself, until I kick it free,

An oscillating arc the jays play under
And the plants suck up, their thirst as great as
Galoots in a cheap saloon.

~

There'll be no breakfast of pancakes and champagne,
Only drainspout coffee on the patio,
Wisp of a cigarette

In a smoky braid with the candle,
Stub of citronella
Lit inside the Chinese lantern, that gray pagoda.

And when the sun steams down
The cruel line of the red horizon, you'll smell
Clouds of mesquite from the supper grill.

I'm homesick for okra, for the bitter greens
Cooked in a cast-iron pot. And I'd like a little mint
To sweeten the bourbon of oblivion.

Let's set the table for burnt crow.
Let's use the big hibiscus for dinner plates,
A sticky stamen in the middle.

Fill all the glasses with that new wine from Albania.
Just pour it in, the way you charge
A battery with acid.

And that fly at prayer
On the rim of the ashtray? Like Pilate,
He's washing his nervous hands of me.

I'm sitting under the stars
Like a ballroom of chandeliers. No wallflower,
No crippled victim of desire,

I dance only
The Cajun Two-Step, the Dirty Shag.
My feet quicken the air like fireflies.

I should be wearing a pith helmet
And canvas pants, a shirt of a thousand pockets—
What's left to discover

But the dark continent of my own heart,
Drumbeat over the dry savanna?
How can I

Return to paradise, the scene of the crime,
If I've never been there before?
Ah Jesus, the night's too hot for philosophy.

Let the rains come, in a rinse of innocence,
Until summer sops up
Whatever the bloated heavens won't hold.

In the Real Verona

A small charge will
let you enter
the house of Juliet and stand
where she looked down,
or would have, had she not been
born of words,
a woman true and false
in a foreign tongue,
and would have seen herself
grown cold
on the stones below the balcony,
fallen from
blood to bronze, her right breast
shining, shining
from every nervous hand
that stroked it
for luck, for love, for all
a touch might mean
when the day stumbles and
light spills
the wrong way around us,
as even now,
and for the same reasons,
where my hand
answers your hot skin,

I feel
a small charge in the dark,
and you let me enter.

Down to Earth

Why should I write about the stars?
They look like the future when it's still
Hot and foreign and far away, before
The cold dose of it arrives, so near
We hear it turn a small doorknob in the dark.

And why moon about the moon? It's not
So gorgeous as I thought: a pocked face
Like a dented hubcap, and bald, with no chin
To speak of, living beyond its means
On the charity of someone else's light.

I need the sluggish tug of mud around
My roots and, overhead, the sleeves of moss
From old oak. Give me a slick lizard
Pumped up on a cedar post, and a mole,
That tiny miner, down in the earth I love.

Even icy limbs that beat like brass knuckles
Against the house can please me, and crickets
Dizzy in the summer dusk. And the rose,
That sweet birthknot of the beautiful, how
Gladly I grasp it in a slash of new thorns.

Half Past August

Milkweed and sneezeweed, a linger of frail wings
(Black and bronze of the Widow Skimmer, lace trim of the
  Mourning Cloak),

And cow tails batting the gnats away like a sultan's slaveboy,
Tassels of tall corn, and heat hazing this country road

I walk by, deep-fried from the sun and salted with sweat,
Downwind from everything that's dead in Ohio, the car, the
  deer,

The last wild thought cooling in my mind, and not ready yet
For the blind worm and the blowfly, that raw debauchery
  inside the soil.

My woozy feet penguin out in front of me, the dust
  wrangling
As a lumber truck sways past, at the end of a log

A red flag beating the air like an open artery, my throat
So thick and dry I could wring the clouds for rain.

Back roads, crossroads, roads that frizzle to the fields
Or slobber down to a ditch. On one side, the rasp of a tractor

Tugging out the rootknots from a stump of old oak. On the
  other,
The rickrack rails of a snake fence keeping in two walleyed
  nags.

How many miles to the next town, a clot of houses
Under the buckeye and the sour gum, deep hypnosis of
  streets

Where I might find a cup of wellwater or a working phone?
Around me, the insolent falsetto of the flies; above, three
  sparrows

Splitting the sky, quick beak and wing, the blue healing after
  them.
Noon long gone, and the day blistering up, I stumble through

The lost summer of myself, stone in the shoe, stone in the
  heart,
As if only each awkward step could take me the slow way
  home.

Another Sunday in the Poconos

Before the others awake,
I own the dawn—
Me, and that fat crow outside the cabin,
Pausing on a small branch
Halfway up the close unnameable tree.
Shakedown artist of the day,
Black wings working
Like some quaint contraption from
The Museum of Industrial Antiques,
He takes his place
On another bough, deeper in the brush,
Barking his raucous cry at the sun.

~

Mist rises and drifts on the gray lake,
Where three men bring
The little trolling motor and its battery
Down to their numbered rowboat, so far away
I see only the silent fuss
Of tackle and jackets on the cool dock.

~

Two swans float by, and two cygnets,
Stiff in the early light, their heads

Gliding through the vapor,
As if they heard, in the back of those mean brains,
Wagner at his most solemn, organ chords
That part the dark
For some lost procession of the dead.

Snapshot with Linguini

Fast film on a slow afternoon, *al fresco,*
Cool tube of the wine bottle
And sweat of olives under the awning,
A shadow taking its own share
Of the beefsteak Florentine, the linguini with garlic and oil,
Not that far down the byways and high walls
From Dante's house, though the only poetry at his namesake
   café
Breathes from the table, and from across the table
Where you subside for once in this long
Babble of Italian, your release
From the arts and altars I bound you to
Before we turned to bed
In the small room, or before we stood
On the narrow balcony
That overlooks the old bridge and overhears the Vespas
Making their run on the banks
Of the Arno from dawn to dawn, as I planned
This day and the next and the next, down to
The first hour of your waking and the last strand of linguini—

It's no wonder
You ease back in your beauty now, this face
No flaking paint or line
Translated from the Middle Ages

Could measure up to, as what but love could
Draw you out and pardon
My clumsy needs, my mean fear of losing
Even one second set aside for
Scheduled revelations in the Tuscan sun, as if
I had not come four thousand miles to find
You framed in the summer light,
This moment when we feel the day float over us
In the lazy grace of its own free will.

Home Truths

Ruins by moonlight, and the swoon
Of waterfalls in a morning mist—
Some must have

Their romance and their dreams
Stamped out
Like cancelled squares in a passport,

Sighing, and checking their sighs
From a handwritten list.
But not even the chapel at Magdeburg,

Where the bowels of dead bishops
Work their crooked miracles,
Can tempt me to

Allegories of the traveler's tale,
Or lessons resurrected from
Ash in a narrow urn.

I've heard that others, seeking
The secrets of a deeper life,
Have pitched their tents

In the shadow of a pyramid, the stars
Gaseous and vast, cramped
As the close sands beneath them,

Listening all night
To the dry music of desert air, the camels
Gnashing their cud from side to side.

I sleep in my own bed,
As noises from the neighborhood
Sift through the screen—

Wet wheels on asphalt,
Crickets with their jackknife knees,
Wind chimes tuned to the blues—

In this city where the only monument's
A bronze of a rubber pioneer
Backed by marble in the courthouse park,

Where there's no
Sacred stone or seventh wonder,
No shrine or reliquary bells,

And the tourists come
By Ram and Storm and Thunderbird
From two towns away,

This midsize city where
Streetlamps steam in the summer heat
And trashbags bulge by the curb,

Where the only ritual's routine,
And tongues of cast brass beat themselves
For birth and work and wakes.

Beurre d'Anjou

From the blue bowl, a pear
Ripe as the belly of some
Pale madonna six months gone.
I touch it warm again, flesh
On flesh, and caress the skin
Blushing like an ingénue, so sweet
With the gold aroma of sun,
Who would need to eat it? And yet

My mouth aches for that taste
Of earth and air and rain, back
To the blossom and the blunt tree
Where it swelled in shade, rounding
From the stem, before it fell through
A slow soft summer to my hands.

By the Waters of Babylon

Under the live oaks, they're pitching camp
At the World Congress of Excitable Ministry,
Each claiming a different day for the earth
To burn, decibel levels like a flashfire
Crinkling the eardrums. Preachers immerse themselves
In a shiver of wet ecstasy, their bad news traveling
At the speed of spit, bluster around the edges, typhoon
On a dead collision course with the wicked.

By the tired waters, near the rooted shore,
The cows look up from their long grass
As if to listen, their lazy tails asleep, their dark eyes
Already doused with boredom of the cud and barn.
The sun's starching out a sky as stiff as
Byzantine saints in a glaze of clay, the day so flat
No one can see through more than two dimensions.

That's no incense from sandalwood, but hickory smoking
From the hocks and ribs, seasoned with a little
Gutter guitar for the cheap seats. They can
Quote you the quotas of heaven, the open door
Policies of hell, and pour salt on all the sweet evils—
Lap dancing in the Blue Goose Lounge; loose shadows
Buttering the multiplex; the sultry torments of rum.

They can work their words to a froth, finding
Asters in disaster and rape in paradise, their tongues
A swarm of syllables in the windy tents, voices
Calling for the sick and crippled, the sore at heart,
Before the backstory of the script, the bottom line:
Send us your innocents, the daughters and the dollars.

And the day steams up like beer over brimstone.
And the river slides down its dirty banks.

Madonnas at Ca' d'Oro

1

I like to think
It's sequence, not circumstance,
These three madonnas

Among the heaven's row of other frames,
A wall of women
Stiff with child, blessed with paint,

In this palace facing
The Grand Canal, its green reek rising
To a loggia of stone,

High enough you can almost believe
The scene's arranged
For looking, the scent vanished

Like the gilt that gave
This house its name, that still glows over
The heads of mother and son.

2

We come on time, but not
On Italian time, the slow doors opening
Past the posted hour.

We go and make our visit, early,
Leaving us free
To take the later train to Padua, talking of Giotto

And that chapel where
We'll see his frail panels of Christ's life,
A Bible story-board

That even the unwashed worshippers
Could read and weep for,
And us among them, dragging our dirty clothes—

The last laundromat in Venice,
That city of incessant water, went out of business
Six months before.

3

Lined up like this,
These three seem a sum of small madonnas
Larger than themselves.

In the first, the infant Jesus fattens
On her virgin breast,
The right one, round as a hungry skull.

The second shows no
Sucking at the tit, though it's exposed,
A globe of white and red.

Mary's modest in the third, dressed to the neck,
But in his hands
The baby cradles an apple, as if to say

Here is my blood,
My mother's milk, a world from which all of us
Have eaten and been weaned.

Crab Festival in Henderson, Louisiana

for Karen

Sweat and rain and the spiced waters
Running down a crab's dead leg—

All morning my sister and I
Kept up with the sun, a junket past Baton Rouge
And over the swills of the Mississippi, the car
Floating on a long bridge through swamps,
Then down a levee road, damp dirt and gravel,
Both of us out for more than
Blue bodies boiled to scarlet, more than
A mouthful of yellow fat, or the sweet white wads inside.

Jaycees and ladies from the church
Roped up the banners, and opened the stands at noon,
Bowls of étouffée and okra gumbo, bottlenecks of beer
Breaking the ice in a washtub, and sno-cones
For the kids, a rainbow drip of syrup
Cool and sticky in the heat.

From the picnic pavilion, over the low-fi speakers,
The keen and fracas of a Cajun fiddle
Pulled us in, my sister sizzling in a two-step,
Fast feet on the concrete floor, before the old folks
Eased out, belly to belly in a bayou waltz,

While I watched, and drained a Dixie, and waited for
That flatbed parked at the end of the pleasure grounds
To rig its traps and mikes, dark faces of a bar band
Pale in the day's deep glare, and then the bass
And drums rumbling from the raw bottom of some R&B,
Smoky sway of a sax that stroked the appetite.

And then a late drizzle under the pines,
Tables sheeted with last week's news, and napkins
Ripped from a roll, where we paid to
Pound a knife handle against hard claws,
And split the cracked mosaic of the lower plates,
And scrape the dead man's chest out with the guts,
Our lips aching with cayenne, spitting back
The bay leaves and the black buckshot of coriander,
Hands wounded by shrapnel on the wet planks,

And all around us, elbow to shoulder, bench after bench,
The homely hierarchies of the South, from rednecks
With a jaw full of Red Man, to the ginghams of gossip,
Seersucker suits from the courthouse seated next to
T-shirts blazoned with heavy metal and the bible camps,
A feast of people busy in the rain, no melting pot,
But a cauldron of crabs baptized in hell, bubbling
And banging under furious water, a rough rite
That savors every lick and sip, even in the mud,
The air still seething with a sultry tang.

Heroic Roses

after a title by Paul Klee

Heroic they'd have to be, the way
I let them struggle.
In this garden, you're on your own.

It's no soap, I tell them,
And no powders, either, nothing
To keep the bugs and blight

Away from the stiff roots, buried
Like a head of startled hair, or off
The new leaves aching upwards to the sun.

Braving the long days, they stand their ground,
Each bud a blood-burst
Of wounded bloom,

Red petals bending back
Until you can see, close inside,
The black heart still beating there—

No, it's a fat bee
Throbbing in the clot, seeking
The deep sweetness of a summer's eve.

No matter how they sway
On those scaly legs, a victim of rickets,
Spindly in the wind,

I never tie them to
Some upright stake; they're always
Free to lash the air.

And when the flowers
Rust and crack, and autumn makes
The limbs more brittle, and turns the leaves to brown,

Even before I take the blades and cut them
Down to earth,
They use the least breeze

To pierce themselves, dead thorns against the stem,
As if too proud to fall
By any sword except their own.

Venice

1

This is the city I came for,
Not phantasms of glass, or tame lace,
Or gilt paving the altar dome,
But the mystery of wet steps
That spread upwards into what—
And the rooms where Ezra
Sank into silence and himself,
Dead when the words went dry.
On that outriding island called after
The angel who paced, hand in hand,
The first fallen out of paradise,
Where all the painted signs point to
Pound and Diaghilev, impresarios
Of the poem and the speaking leap,
I lost myself among
The tombs and monuments, needing
Another gardener to guide me
To the green grave, an oval
With no more than his name
Flat on the inset plate, a plot
That simplified his life
In the swaying shade of the trees.
And though I stood stiff, the wind
Blew me all the way back

To that small square I sat in
The afternoon before, the bench
Facing an old wall on which
Bronze tablets told in bold relief
The harrowing of Jews dragged out
From the narrow maze, the ache
And angry ash of the deathcamps
Breaking the leafmeal peace
Of the *campo ghetto nuovo*, drowning
Even the noise of two Italian teenagers
Not ten feet behind me, playing
A crude radio in a wooden box,
Homemade ghetto-blaster wired in
To some unseen source of energy,
The scald of black rap
Coming down hard
On the bottom line of rhymes.

2

Sea air and the acids
Smoked over from the inland mills
Still pour against
The stone features of a face
And blunt them. This saint
Or civic hero, this snubnose mariner
Or moneybags with a weak chin
And an itch for immortality,
Comes each year closer to
The young leper king of Jerusalem,
Who won the agonizing shrines

In bloodbought battles and lost
His hold on flesh, staking the cross
For the landlord coffers of Christendom.
Whoever he was, this head
Fixed over an ancient entranceway,
The naming planes now slack
And the juttings dull, he feels
Less and less himself with every breeze,
Leaving, in the slow rub
And lessons of the weather, a look
That brings us backward to
The human mud we all were cast from.

3

Rising on the slip
And slap of water, locked off
From passages that foreign feet
Bull through—a labyrinth of alleys
Where the Jew and Moor
Found no profit in
Their torchlit tales—the houses have
No business being upright
In this late age, with little
Steadfast underneath to shoulder them
And take the strain. The tides
Sweep in the freedom
Of the evening sea, and ebb away
Blood souvenirs of greed and breathless love,
A gold grain in the backwash
As the day fades down

Over stone and marble, deep shadows
Rinsing the doorways and panes
Until the palace walls all fall
Dark enough for kissing and for death.

4

After the lapse of six years,
We walk out again
From the guidebooks to the square,
Scaffolds still propping up
The brow of that basilica
Shipped in with distant trade,
Like the body of its namesake saint
Smuggled here in a pork barrel,
Greek and Gothic and Saracen, gold making
Its old devotions to the sun,
Perpetual vows
Always under repair. A breeze lifts
From the green lagoon, and carries
Over us the white noise of crowds,
Somewhere behind it
An easy stroke of oars
Wimpling the water. We don't feed
The pigeons posing for the scrapbook,
Or pay the summer premium
For drinks squeezed down on a table
The size of a pizza pan, sticky with
The stale showtunes and jazz
A band melts over the hush of dusk,

Before the moon turns
Even these cheesy themes to love.
Under the dark arcade whose windows
Glisten with silver, with crystal
That wears its heart on a tag, on whose steps
The rootless offspring of Europe
Plant the garish bracken of their backpacks,
We pause for a long look
At the towers of clock and bell, the palace
Pink in the postcard night.
Around us, the streets veer
And weave and lose themselves
In a blind of bridges and damp doors,
Each corner keeping
Its own secrets as we stroll,
Mapping a dry way out.
All I want can be found in
The innuendoes of stone, annals
Balanced between the gilt
And the garbage, an afterloom
In the tourist eye. This is
The city I was born for,
Bride-sigh of the Adriatic, widow
Swanking the cleavage in her weeds,
Patched and powdered and pressed
For luck, dream relieving dream,
The way a floodrace overtakes
The undertow, and the starstained waves
Raise their luster back to loss.

On or about the Feast of Saint Absentia

Leaves like the russet of robins
Before the fall, brought down
By a swat of wind in the oak boughs.
Past midnight, and the sewer rats
Creep out, experts on catastrophe, reckless
In the mutilated light, a local wisdom
Prowling the lampposts and flowerweeds,
On a bicker of small claws.

Only one bird's left against the dark
And the tyranny of silence, another
Wounded genius who can't hold
His liquor or his tongue, a tune
Too barbarous for art, in this night
Where a lean moon moves among the stars,
Starving in that appetite for black,
That long receding dazzle of oblivion.

At dawn, all the winesaps wear white
From the sorcery of frost, and shaken silver
Plates the deep pockets of the rose. Inside,
A woman, supple in her sleep, still trembling
From the aftertouch of dreams, rises to
A glitter like a shrine banked with candles—
New sun on the window, melting the rime,
A little slip of rills in the permanent.

The Runes, the Brute Remedies

1

Leaves down, and day down, and mercury
At home in the cold measure,
In the buried bulb.

All afternoon, a low shoal of clouds
Rippled across the sky,
Flow of hearsay on the westering waters.

It's a long fall from the roadside sumac
With its burnt blooms,
The rusty oaks, the tree of heaven cast out,

And a far stretch to the milkweed, and lilies
On their tall stalks,
Barefoot ambitions in the air.

We open the book of oblivion, the runes
Of ruin, thumbed over
In the end time,

Almanac of snow from the moon, season
Of the blood sacrifice,
A good month

To screw the lid down tight on words
Preserved in vinegar,
Pickled in the brine of our own sweat.

2

Veterans Day, and the flags stiff, the halyards rattling,
A breeze blowing hard from
No man's land—

In memory, we perfect the dead,
Fetish and relic
In the brittle ministry of the mind.

And then the sun cuts through November
Hazing the gray, a blade
Cleaning itself in the lover's wound,

And we suck in the rumors of breath,
The light
Infinity wastes on our tired faces,

Fire with nowhere to cling but the broken
Branches in the grate,
As if that mattered to us now,

As if we were not summoned to the dark
By our own dumb voices—
Hush of shadow, threshold of stone.

E-Mail to William in Wales

for William Greenway

No heathens in the heather here. In fact, no heather, only a
last stand of goldenrod and red leaves dismantled from the
maple. Our seasons feel the same, though the hours are
slow to cross the cold ocean: your moon benighted, our
day a half-lap behind the zodiac.

Are they still preaching down the pit mines, in those wet
towns you travel through? Do the little ponies pray in
their tack and snaffle, or still lick sugar from a druid's
hand? Does the black air echo with hymns and whinnies,
holy singalongs by the coalface? Here, the brays of evan-
gelists could drive a mule to suicide.

Long walks in the mire, in the stony vales, must strop your
appetite. But what, in that land of the unpronounceable
and the indigestible, do you dare to eat? Thank heaven for
Betty and her soups, and for Swansea of the pubs and the
tub-thumping poet, where stout will warm the weird
dishes you struggle to keep down, as all petitions to the
kitchen gods go up in greasy smoke.

I can see the evening rise around you, midges like a puff of
molecules on the damp horizon. Inside the cottage that
vines cover like a week's growth of whiskers, you toss your

boots in the mud room and poke the lazy fire, easing your Georgia bones to the armchair, on one side a dry glass of gin floating an olive with its nipple of pimento, on the other side the lines you pull from your prophetic beard, no antilyrics of analysis, but music sweet as a bosomy rose and strict as the bedrock of death and its grim satisfactions.

Everything creaks after the hard freeze, grisaille of winter one minute before the dawn. I've had those mornings, too, when you double-clutch the toilet handle and hotwire the coffeepot, sump pump of your heart bringing the blood up to a sluggish level. And then sunlight splinters the tight sky, and steam lifts from the heavy cup, and you walk out again where the world softens under your feet.

I send my greetings through the ether to Nigel who, at that party in Youngstown, for a moment put down his politics and picked up a blues harp, the wail of Wales in a wicked idiom; and to the ghost of Dylan, still thundering along the strand where the waves break and shudder. Is it his spirit that holds you there? You've been gone since the first bellflower inched up from the rich Ohio earth and rang its angelus, and now the last cosmos leans over and drops its delicate petals. William, come home.

Solstice of the Goat

November: geese with a head start on the snow,
And leaves like a slaughter of innocents . . .

Winter we know by rote, as if we lived
Above the tree line crippled in ice.

We've seen the signs. Chickadees hang hard
To the rancid fat; pigs drip from the black branches.

And the dogs, high bred or hybrid, are putting on
New coats, keeping their heat close to the bone.

And that's it for the turkey, the table set for grace.
The car turns over once and quits, acid low in the holes.

And the market's down again, like frightened mercury.
Prayer won't help, though you can't tell that

To the Reverend Mincewit, with his forgery of bells,
Big tongues licking at the brazen lips.

The season sends the wrong news, the sun
No more than hearsay in a rumor of heaven.

And what does that leave us, on this bitter street?
Rickets of oak, ribcage of maple;

Wind like a chest wound sucking air;
The mind suspended by its own meat hook.

In our dreams, we're sleeping under goatskin,
Wolf pelts for pillows and grease on the belly,

Like brutes from a north of fog and no fire,
In a blue-veined country of cold blood.

Postcards from Iberia

for William and Betty Greenway

1

In Bilbao, the skin of the new museum
Glistered in moonlight and glowed
Like billions of bullion under the sun.
Eyes shaken, I stood on the terrace
Where it landed, alien mothership of the arts,
Voluptuous wreck
In a languor of angles and wry curves, stuck
By the ugliest river in Spain.

2

Underground, in the labyrinth between
The green line and the red line,
I felt the sly fingers
In my pocket, pesetas on the way out,

When I yelled, and William leaped in,
Two poets of middle age against
The quick thieves,
Jumpcut and strobe light of memory

Leaving nothing but the legends of wrestle
And cash in my hand,

The aftershocks
Of warfare too sudden for fear.

Ah, Barcelona, we came up from the dark
To your sinister chimneys, the charm
Of seasick facades,
Dragon spines over the rooftop,

And broken tiles that recongregate
In the tall spires of
An absent god,
City of the long ramble and the short fuse.

3

Inside the museum, where *The Garden of Delights*
Stared down *The Triumph of Death*
Across the room, among the silent crowds,

Both busy in their chronicles
From the bad apple to the fierce bone,
I found myself

Coming back to the Black Paintings of Goya,
To the head of that dog
Lost in a desert of dry oils,

Nothing so sweetly hopeless
As the look he gave me, left behind
Forever in that heavy frame.

4

We took the tour bus to the top
Of Toledo, a view stretching steep
As El Greco's emaciated wavers,
A loose troop lagging through
The stone cathedral, a Moorish colonnade
In the synagogue of the white madonna,
And the shops of gimcrack and damascene,
Where I bought my own blade, forged
In authentic steel, and keen enough
For villains or for paring cheese.

5

Even at the airport, that odor,
And somewhere in the sultan's garden
That same scent, bringing me back
To my boyhood and the strong
Solutions my mother used in her permanent—

Who would have thought the Alhambra
So close to the South I'd lived in, so far
From these towers and fountains, this palace
Whose arches open to a space like caves,
Crusts of plaster dripping from the dome?

On the terrace of the parador, I could smell
In the evening breeze the essence of Granada—
Roses large and soft as a cat's head; that lime

Plucked from the hillside path; a spice of olives
Soaked in their own oil; wet attar of the Arab night.

6

All the stolen gold of the Indies
Seems to mummify that high altar
Where, on Corpus Christi, the small boys
Dance in their cassocks and castanets,
Beyond the stiff procession of the pallbearers
Shouldering the tomb of Columbus, one more
Accessory of death in the dim cathedral—

Sevilla of white and gold-ocher, orange trees
Trimmed square against the fortress walls,
Not far from the silky river that flows
By bullring and opera house, same circle
In the same colors of earth and sun—

City where the boughs of pink orchids
Crest on a spiny trunk, where we posed
In the Garden of Poets, where we leaned against
The blues of plumbago and morning glory
Pouring down a corner of the Casa de Pilatos,
Where we sopped our churros in chocolate
And dined on wild hare and venison
In *mozarabe* sauce, our last meal

Before a taxi raced the dawn
Through rainy streets and aromatic air,

Speeding us from the slow delirium
Of Spain, where all we failed to do,
In the tired hours of our travel, gave us
A thousand green reasons to return.

Flu Season, Says the Almanac

Permission to be sick, sir. Or rather,
The permission sickness gives you, not some
Bone-curling disease that makes the future
Bend back on itself, but the woozy
Afterblur of flu, fever enough to keep you home
One more day from bad coffee and the boss:

Indolence of the ill, a pampering of clean pajamas
And hours free to watch a dozen channels
All at once, part juggler, part jazzbo
Improvising medleys on the black remote,
From rappers to wrestlers to the perfect marriage
Of tuna and arugula, fingers still supple
Among the gawky pleasures of the shut-in.

Too old or distant for a mother's touch,
You nurse your own wet nose, mopping up
Self-pity with every sneeze, God bless you.
And there's nothing the doctor can do
You can't do for yourself, dosing
The parasites with drugs and orange juice,
As if all of you were on holiday together
On some hot fruity island of the Maladies.

It's not so bad, alone under the weather
And a cloudy quilt, as long as you can see
At the other end of ache, beyond
The bedridden breath and rheumy solitude,
A leisure that allows a separate life
To idle until it ripens, a small lull
Before the busy work of being you again.

Nahum

for Lynn Powell

Well, the Lord's just furious
About Nineveh, so mad He could
Have His way in a whirlwind and
Suck them up like dust. And what's
Nineveh to Him or He to Nineveh,
That He should be so pissed? Well,
They're just plain wicked, that's what,
Even unto the young children,
Who shall be dashed down from
High places, and the whole city
Trampled under chariots, hub to hub
In a hubbub of streets—no end to
Corpses when the Lord's at work,
And no second chance. He'll pull
The skirts of the harlot over her face
And show the nations her nakedness,
Though that's just how the whore
Came to trouble in the first place.
And that noise you hear? Well,
It's either the sting of the whip
Or a clatter of knees smiting together.
And all this shall He do because
They are vile, they are heathen, they are

Spoiled meat for the cankerworm.
O Nineveh, this time you've really
Gone and done it, evil up to the ears.
And none shall look back on thee,
And none find thee anywhere but in
The bloody chapters of this little book.

Airs for Oboe and Snare

1

The sickbed breath of November
Curls up the dead end of leaves
And blows the light out by five o'clock.
All day the sun beat down on this
Quick drum of earth, and now the cold
Comes back again, like a spectral whisper
Through the woodwinds. I pull the coat
Closer, snug inside my own bony night.

2

The leaves mound here like fresh graves
In which we've buried the season.

The city crews, with their trucks and rakes,
Sweep up each heap along the curb.

Bad back and weak will, I paid
Somebody else to clean the autumn lawn,

Sweat and muscle hired by the hour, strapped
To loud machines that do the wind's work.

3

In the unzoned country, they still burn
The trash of trees—bonfire of maple,
Barbecue of oak, leaves the color of flame
Before the first match spurts. Driving down
The dusk of back roads, I've seen that
Lick and swagger, spasm and smear, spark
Spilling upwards into wisp, like a sacrifice
Of love letters the night before a battle.

4

Limbus of crystal on the bare limbs;
Crickets on the fritz; gray sun like a scab
On a sky that may never heal. A field mouse
Glistens its way against the frail trinkets of ice.

Through the low stobs and offal, hound
And hunter crunch, scaring up the birds
The gun brings down, a slur rumpling
From the dog's mouth, hot slobber and sprawl.

5

Leaf by leaf, the world goes to ground.
And flake by flake, it sidles back,
Colder now, ghost of itself, in a light
So hard and sharp it prints on every pane
A wintry crop of snowrose and frostflower,
Through which my stubborn eye looks past,
Eccentric lens, to see the trees bristle
And bees stitch the garden together again.

For the Shepherds at Bethlehem

What were they thinking,
Spooked when the angels spoke, a sudden
Choir of light in the raw sky? I'd have them think:

Thank God, God wasn't born in Gomorrah,
Bad start in some burnt-out ruin among
The ashes of cats and the wicked bones. And thank God,
It's Bethlehem, town of the pretty name,
Just down the stony hills from here
To a stable where the ox and the ass
Feel at home, big teeth cracking the grain,
And a jawful of straw to cleanse the palate.

I'd have them kneel
Around the odd family, staring at
The birthblood bright on the robes
Of a pale girl, and the tired man beside her
Worrying his whiskers with a helpless hand,
And the alien baby in the hay.

One of them would take from his leather pouch
A supper of olives and flatbread, something
Salty to gnaw on and share. And one,
By accident, would knock his staff
Against the shaky manger, waking the child

From a troubled sleep. And one of them,
Hearing that cry in the night's chill,
Would lift a lamb to the infant's face, new wool
Greasing it against the cold, calming
The baby in the dark. And I'd have them

Rise from the rough silence and prod their herds
Back to the field, uneasy and relieved, having found
Whatever it was they'd come for,
The air so loud with bleats, so busy with
Gossip among the flocks, that no one would
See that high enormous star
Sliding its light across the cloudy sheep.

Where I Stand

Many have been to Ohio, but none
Has ever returned. Do I mean
Returned to Ohio, or returned
Wherever they came from? It's too hard
To think standing here on an iceberg.
The feet are the first to go, a blue creep
Up to the knees, and north of the knees,
Until the brain floats frozen
On this river of mystery and doubt,
A river the thoughts cross over
One small floe at a time, leaping
And stumbling and plunging in.

And who are these people who want
To go to Ohio? And why won't they leave,
Or why won't they ever return? You'll get
No answers out of me, standing here
On this cracked puzzle of a river,
Scratching my head till the iceflakes fall
Down to the knees, and south of the knees,
The snow of my own mind

Blown back by the whiplash wind,
Howling around me like a cold
Gust of ghosts, drifting halfway between
The shackles and the broken shore.

Postpartum Blues

Soon the glass angel must be
Wrapped and packed and put away,
And this hard year swept out
Like tinsel from the Christmas tree—
The end of December, aromatic
In its homely smoke, and the thin limbs
Of maple and ash, the pipecleaner pines,
Brushing themselves against
The cold carbons of evening.

I've watched the ice turn
Little knifeblades in the grass.
Sly beneath them, the mole
Knows what to do with dirt—
Shoulder it aside, crumb by claw,
And build a city deep,
A labyrinth of dark
Under the stone and the root.
I think I could live there.

I think I could make
A music of my own. Thinking
Makes a music of its own.
You can hear it when
Some stray phrase stumbles down

The rabbit hole, a few words
That broke from the brain
And won't go back, always
One step ahead of the real.

But what's in the way
To the way in? God,
That desperate explanation,
Mentor and tormentor, giving us
The duties of paradise,
Obligations of the saved?
And is my way in
This abyss of the belly, where they
Tied the first knot in my life?

Even the virgin must have felt
The postpartum blues, crazy enough
To pin sweet curls in her hair,
Shavings she picked up from
The floor of the carpenter's shop.
I think I can still hear
The baby wailing. Or is that cry
The dead beating on their graves
For the earth to open—

And to let them out, or to let us in?

Blizzard near Emporia, 1893

That winter so mean we took the mule in
To the schoolhouse and rumped him up aside the stove,
He didn't stink no worse than the rest of them
And was just as smart. Look here, Miss Honeydew said,
You can't leave that animal around all day. Look out,
We said, this mule's all we got, and the snow's already
Heaped up way past the hay bales, and the water won't crack.
It's fixing to snow till it's done, and it ain't near done yet.
Any fool can see that, Miss Honeydew said, and I'm no fool.
No ma'm, we said, but it's warm in here, and dry,
And even a mule can't breathe under snow. Old Reuben
Done like to froze when the wind hit him, and it won't
Get no better before it gets worse. Nobody going nowhere
Nohow in this storm, and that's a lesson to us all.
And that little Jenkins kid piped up: I know that mule.
Caught him down in the corn some months back, and my
    daddy
Had to beat him off with a scarecrow. That's the mule,
We said, but there ain't nothing in here to eat but books,
And he ain't got a taste for them yet—and neither has you,
Young Jenkins, if everything your mama says is true.
All right, all right, Miss Honeydew said, any creature's
Welcome in a blizzard, as long as I'm running things.
And that's when Reuben let out his piss like a frayed rope,
So loud on the bare boards you couldn't hear the wind.

That happens, we said. A mule's like to do that any time.
Must be the stove thawed him out down to the piss.
A good floor will take that without no trouble, if it
Was laid down right to begin with, and this one was—
We put it in ourselves, flat and snug, two hot summers ago.
Miss Honeydew shoved and scraped her desk some feet away
And looked at Old Reuben and looked to the window.
You might want to take him out back right now, she said,
Before he thaws out any more. This room's a schoolhouse,
Not an outhouse. And we have work to do
Before the light goes. Ma'am, we said, work is
Something we know all about, and so does this mule.
But nobody works when the snow's this high. And
Where's a mule to go in a storm like this, when the wind
Hangs up in his hide like barb wire? Let it slack a bit,
And we'll haul him home, if the house ain't disappeared.
Miss Honeydew poked Old Reuben's haunch with a yardrule
Till he backed hisself into a corner; his long ears stood up
Sorrowful, like some dunce. We'd never seen a mule
Look so ashamed. Well, said Miss Honeydew, just so
He keeps himself quiet and clean. We thank you, ma'am,
We said, for this kindness, and Reuben thanks you, too.
And outside, the world went blind and lame, teaching us
A thing or two about the place of mules, stuck here in this
Godforsaken state where winter comes on so hard and wild
No one can miss the point, not even that half-wit Jenkins boy.

In the Zone of Perpetual Weather

Let us not talk about the weather.

—SAMUEL JOHNSON

After the last caul of ice
Crackling on the black branches, on the bare grass,
The season gives itself away—
Crocus up, and snowdrops before them, and before long
A sun that pulls
New heat from the mull of mud, and frees
The frozen sleepers from their bad dreams. And whose song,
As April breaks from the bone
In a spool of music, a plunge of seed,
Whose song would you prefer: cricket or cicada?
Shrill leap
Into the here and now, crazy castanets of the wing;
Or the wish for a split life,
High drone of escape into later? No, no—
It's the unknown I want,
Whatever's silent around me, and stubborn
Beyond the stones:
Dark light of desire
Breeding itself in the dead leaves.

Inside the Walls of Avila

We walked from church to church, the tour guide
Speaking in Spanglish
Over our whole busload of foreign tongues,

You lagging sometimes behind, sometimes with me,
A loose end
Down the narrow wallway of stone streets.

All through the mountains from Madrid, you said
Little that morning,
Looking at the steep green plunge we rode so close to.

And what was there to say, drowsing above
The tires' drone
And under the gray glide of storks in the spring sky?

Camera in its black case aching from my neck,
I took time
To quicken that slow city to a standstill.

Now three photographs alone frame that day for me:
The small square
With its statue of San Juan de la Cruz,

Pale poet and saint, who saw the soul embracing God
Like a lover
Lost in the dark pent-up ecstasies of flesh;

And that gaudy altar, in the church of her childhood home,
Where Santa Teresa
Shone in gold, baroque among the holy bric-a-brac;

And you smiling near that high wide gate, the noonday
Sun pouring through,
And the wind, with its soft hands, brushing your hair.

Springlines

Cardinals like a heartskip in the snowcapped cedar,
Jays with their Mohawks and screech—

But no spring until the robin strides across the lawn,
Puffed up like a banker in his red vest.

~

Here, in the flatlands, we measure our rise and fall
From the mountain laurel to the mountain ash.

~

Even in April, a spray of snow on the new grass, and ice
Seducing the sidewalk, as if nature had said: Why don't you
Slip into something a little more uncomfortable?

~

On the kitchen table, daffodils drop feet first in a glass
Of clear water, a straggle of stems sucking it up.

Along the rock path, tulips shake their blowzy heads,
A line of one-legged women with a raucous laugh.

~

After the night in ruins, dilapidations of the dew,
We walk out again, leaves blowing all around us,
Green in the loose breeze, not ferries poled over
To the underworld, but small boats floating on the air,
Bearing us back across a slow river of light.

~

Crow, by any other name, means blood money,
Means cyanide tattoo, means tongue of barbed wire.

~

In the rainlicked afternoons, something seems to whisper
Innuendoes for the inner ear, tender obscenities,
Until we want to lie down in a bed of mud
And watch the frail flowers unbutton themselves.

~

Dogwoods, on the dark side of the house, give up the ghost,
Ghost of a cold month summoned by a séance of clouds—
All those white petals stabbed in the heart.

~

That small shrub, that dwarf, that little fuckup in the garden,
Won't bloom for weeks, dozing into June, and even then
Puts out only a few insolent fingers of pink.

Spring with its toys and accessories; spring in the dead
   windows
Of Omaha and Dubuque; spring when the last smoke of
   winter
Curls up inside the chimney, and pollen finds its way out,
Spilling everywhere, like sawdust from a rag doll's head.

In one sudden hour, the air broke from flurries
To a lacquer of sunlight on the hard sky.

It's easy now to brush away the dander of pear and crab,
Like a janitor in the school gym, after the spirit rally.

It's easy to forget that long March, naked and foreign and
   starved,
Down to this trance of mock orange, this open circus of
   birds.

Exhausted from false alarms, we've come to believe in blue
   again,
And a future that always arrives too late, and by surprise.

Half-Numb from Winter,
on a Morning Almost Warm

Go for wisdom to the iris, beard
Like a Chinese sage
In a flutter of philosophy.
Let the tall tongue of the iris
Tell you what spring is—
Root of the rainbow; waterfall pouring itself
Into itself; cloud-rot before
The cautery of sun
Burning the season clean again.

How would the trees know, small leaves
In a spray of green wind?
Or the grass gone wild with rain? You can't hear
What the fat bees hum, too low for words.
And whatever the weeds say,
Don't listen.

Go ask the iris what spring means,
Thrusting up from its dirty heart.

Latter Days

Now, in April, the evenings longer with light,
And a lingering chill of winter on the heart,
The night flows in, low to the ground, like spreading juniper,

And at the end of the avenue, a moon enormous in the sky,
Color of stale champagne, always turning the same face to us,
Pale glow we can count on, lean or full.

Those boughs so lately bent beneath a slouch of snow
Lift and whisper through their new leaves, as if they could
Romance the wind and sweet-talk the furies into peace.

I know that voice, though it was never mine. I need
Gravel on the tongue to give my words some traction,
Or they'll slip to easy speech, with no wit or weight.

I envy Adam, name-dropping among the glamorous animals,
And those who first found in plants a likeness they could
Call out in common words, as *mullein* came to *candlewick*.

What can we christen now, in this language of the hand-me-
    down,
From myth to mouth? The cold lake, cracked open weeks ago,
Gushes from a pure spring, and small birds drink deep from it.

Cognac and a stiff-necked lamp, and beside me
The beast of solitude with its dirty paws, still reeking of
Fresh meat beneath the ribs, teeth grinding while I think . . .

Back in those early years, I was never fit for silk pavilions
Or sherbet in a silver cup. Even peasants who live on turnip
  soup
And sleep under straw with their pig and geese and kids

Seemed too good for me. But I could root like that hog,
If I had to, down on all fours in the duff, nosing out
Nuts and truffles on a forest floor, fat Columbus of the grunt.

Now the new stars look in and find me here, housebroken,
Head aslant, in a wintry skin, the soft touch of my vowels
No more than lost quotations from the mockingbird.

Who but a fool believes there's something tragic in
What has to happen, exile or ice or the end of love? The
  daffodils
Still sway in black air, their only grace to be graceful.

These days, these nights peeled back to the past, I make no
Arguments against the dark, but listen to my daughter's
  damaged pet,
The little blind dog that barks as the sun goes down.

Here and Hereafter

God chooses punishment but I choose the crime.

—RICHARD CECIL

If, by some black miracle, I found myself
A saint, who would believe me
One of the thinner innocents,
Haggard for God, with no more hunger than
The ghost of a hummingbird, dining for three days
On a drop of dew and the red scent of thistle?

Birds and brides and other martyrs of the taut belly
May pride themselves on a bowl of grain,
A green stew and a root, sucking their cheeks
Down to impeccable bone,
Eclipse of flesh by the shadows of the famished,

But I'm more swayed by
Pigmeat and bons mots, biscuits I can't resist
And words that fit the mouth, a sigh of thighs
And the fat bottom of the artichoke.
I sing for my supper
With a tuning fork and musical spoons,
Tenor of the rabbity appetite, prepared to live
Not by bread alone, but also
By butter, by berries in cream, by the season's feast—

Meals of melon in the phosphor of August,
Catfish in the cool of Lent.

Whatever my tongue turns to—
Tobacco's hazy taste, or the braid of forbidden syllables,
The peatsmoke smell of a single malt,
Or unwashed women bathed in the odors of love—
I know there'll always be, after the damp underside
Of Saturdays debauched and drained,
A Sabbath of reassessment, pardon and penance before
The next hard plunge, as if
The prodigal kept coming back, forgiven each week,
Veal on the kitchen planks, and a crock of pale wine.

The priest with his altered ego; the spinster
Wringing the sour sweat from her gown; philosophers
Of the old school, men of distinctions,
Splitting the hairs on a hair shirt—
What solace is there in misery, what joy
Without the sops and revels of the dark sublime?
If you feather the truth to a fine finish,
It's too slick to hold on to.

I'm no Moses on a mountain top, no mad prophet
Pulling his whiskers and bringing the stone tablets down,
A dish of gristle for the backsliding tribes.
I'm no scold of any testament, no crazed reformer
Like that crackpot Saul, knocked for a loop
On the low road to Damascus, a baldheaded man

Getting back up on his high horse, giving himself
A new name and a new mission.

The nine Beatitudes, the fourteen Stations of the Cross—
All those whole and holy numbers leave me numb,
My mind in a panic, like a duck
Trapped in a galvanized bucket, banging his beak on the rim.
What white steeple would I love more than
The pink of spring's own bud and bloom, the blue of
    autumn
Transparent through the empty trees?
Why would I gamble on the absolute, when I have here
The purple evidence of plums, the testimony of wild
    persimmon?

This hand I'm holding in the game of chance
Won't change, not now, with the last card drawn
And everything I am laid on the table.
Is there some secret luck I'll never know about,
Some deep sleeve that buttons up the bet?
Who cares if the odds are honest? When all the stiff-eyed
Kings are dead and the queen of spades buried,
You play the ace, and I'll play the fool.